This book belongs to

_____

Dear Santa Claus,
I know you're busy so
I'll make this short.
Please bring a puppy.
-Patient Ninja

Hi Santa,

I've been really good this year, I mean kinda. I only, cut my little sister's hair and got into a fight with her one time a day. So I was wondering, would you bring me a baby wolf?

Thanks, Unplugged Ninja

Dear Santa,
I would really like it if you helped all the kids who don't have families, find one.
Yours truly,
Grateful Ninja

12 Days of Christmas

By Mary Nhin

Pictures by
Jelena Stupar

On the first day of Christmas, the Ninjas gave to me...

a vacation to the beach.

On the second day of Christmas, the Ninjas gave to me...

2 ice cream cones,
and a vacation to the beach.

On the third day of Christmas, the Ninjas gave to me...

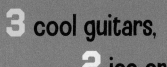3 cool guitars,

2 ice cream cones,

and a vacation to the beach.

On the fourth day of Christmas, the Ninjas gave to me...

4 speedy bikes,   2 ice cream cones,
3 cool guitars,   and a vacation to the beach.

On the fifth day of Christmas, the Ninjas gave to me...

cheesy
fries!

4 speedy bikes,   **2** ice cream cones,

3 cool guitars,   and a vacation to the beach.

On the sixth day of Christmas, the Ninjas gave to me...

6 skateboards strolling,
5 cheesy fries,
4 speedy bikes,
3 cool guitars,
2 ice cream cones,

and a vacation to the beach.

On the seventh day of Christmas, the Ninjas gave to me...

7 puppies dancing,
6 skateboards strolling,
5 cheesy fries,
4 speedy bikes,

3 cool guitars,
2 ice cream cones,
and **a** vacation to the beach.

On the eighth day of Christmas, the Ninjas gave to me...

8 goldfish swimming,
7 puppies dancing,
6 skateboards strolling,
5 cheesy fries,

4 speedy bikes,
3 cool guitars,
2 ice cream cones,
and a vacation to the beach.

On the ninth day of Christmas, the Ninjas gave to me...

On the tenth day of Christmas, the Ninjas gave to me...

On the eleventh day of Christmas, the Ninjas gave to me...

11 lizards singing,
10 drones flying,
9 books a-leaping,
8 goldfish swimming,
7 puppies dancing,

6 skateboards strolling,
5 cheesy fries,
4 speedy bikes,
3 cool guitars,
2 ice cream cones,

and a vacation to the beach.

On the twelfth day of Christmas, the Ninjas gave to me...

12 balls a-bouncing,
11 lizards singing,
10 drones flying,
9 books a-leaping,
8 goldfish swimming,
7 puppies dancing,

6 skateboards strolling,
5 cheesy fries,
4 speedy bikes,
3 cool guitars,
2 ice cream cones,
and a vacation to the beach.

Check out our Ninja Life Hacaks Box Sets or download freebies at ninjalifehacks.tv

@marynhin @GrowGrit
#NinjaLifeHacks

Mary Nhin Grow Grit

Grow Grit

ninjalifehacks.tv

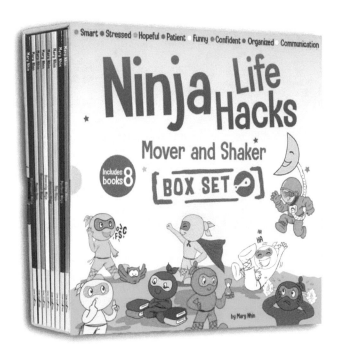

Smart • Stressed • Hopeful • Patient • Funny • Confident • Organized • Communication

Ninja Life Hacks
Mover and Shaker
Includes 8 books
[BOX SET]

by Mary Nhin

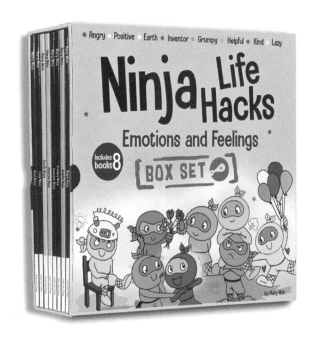

Angry • Positive • Earth • Inventor • Grumpy • Helpful • Kind • Lazy

Ninja Life Hacks
Emotions and Feelings
Includes 8 books
[BOX SET]

by Mary Nhin

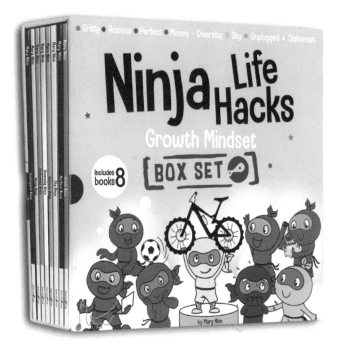

Gritty • Anxious • Perfect • Money • Diversity • Shy • Unplugged • Dishonest

Ninja Life Hacks
Growth Mindset
Includes 8 books
[BOX SET]

by Mary Nhin

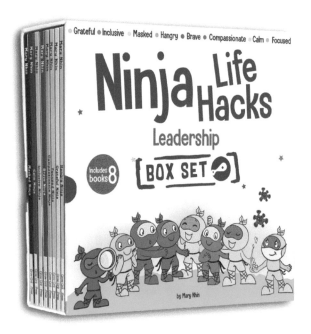

Grateful • Inclusive • Masked • Hangry • Brave • Compassionate • Calm • Focused

Ninja Life Hacks
Leadership
Includes 8 books
[BOX SET]

by Mary Nhin

Hi Santa,

I've been really good this year, I mean kinda. I only, cut my little sister's hair and got into a fight with her one time a day. So I was wondering, would you bring me a baby wolf?

Thanks, Unplugged Ninja

Dear Santa Claus,
I know you're busy so I'll make this short. Please bring a puppy.
-Patient Ninja

Dear Santa,
I would really like it if you helped all the kids who don't have families. find one.
Yours truly.
Grateful Ninja

Printed in the USA
CPSIA information can be obtained
at www.ICGtesting.com
LVHW061505121223
766149LV00020B/1321